Contents

Harnessing the power of the wind

Wind is a valuable source of energy. People have used the wind for centuries to drive mills and pumps, and more recently to power modern turbines. Most importantly, wind is a renewable resource: it will never run out. We can harness it to produce electricity, and wind power has become increasingly important in the twenty-first century.

Wind is air on the move. It is caused by the the Sun, which is the original source of all the world's energy. Solar heat warms some parts of the Earth more than other parts, and this affects the blanket of air that surrounds our planet. For example, land areas heat up more quickly than the sea, but they also cool down more quickly. As air becomes warmer, it expands and rises. Nearby cooler air then flows in to replace the warm air, in a process called circulation.

Winds of the world

There is a pattern to the world's wind circulation. In the tropical region near the equator, where both the land and the sea are hottest, warm air rises and cooler air moves in to replace it. This movement of air creates the trade winds, which take their name from the fact that they once powered merchant sailing ships. The trade winds usually blow from east to west because of the rotation of the Earth, which deflects them.

Further away from the equator, there are bands of westerly winds caused by surface air reaching an area that spins more slowly

Land and sea breezes

Why is it usually breezy at the coast? The reason is that during the day the land is warmer so air rises above it. Cooler air comes off the sea to replace it, causing an onshore sea breeze. At night, the land cools faster than the sea, and air generally flows off the land, creating an offshore land breeze. This small repeating pattern of air circulation is a good example of how winds form.

ENERGY

Wind Power

Neil Morris

W
FRANKLIN WATTS
LONDON • SYDNEY

An Appleseed Editions book

First published in 2009 by Franklin Watts
338 Euston Road, London NW1 3BH

Franklin Watts Australia
Hachette Children's Books
Level 17/207 Kent St, Sydney, NSW 2000

© 2009 Appleseed Editions

Created by Appleseed Editions Ltd,
Well House, Friars Hill, Guestling,
East Sussex TN35 4ET

Designed by Helen James
Edited by Mary-Jane Wilkins
Artwork by Guy Callaby
Picture research by Su Alexander

ISBN 978 07496 8776 2

Dewey Classification: 333.9'2

A CIP catalogue for this book is available from the British Library.

Photograph acknowledgements
page 8 Ashley Cooper/Corbis; 10 Frans Lemmens/Zefa/Corbis; 11 Richard T Nowitz/
Corbis; 12 Macduff Everton/Corbis; 15 Tom Bean/Corbis; 17 Copyright The Poul La
Cour Museum, Askov,Denmark; 20 Ingo Wagner/epa/Corbis; 21 Anthony West/
Corbis; 22 Chinch Gryniewicz; Ecoscene/Corbis; 23 Lowell Georgia/Corbis; Murat
Taner/Zefa/Corbis; 27 Ingo Wagner/DPA/Corbis; 29 Siemens Press Picture; 31 Gideon
Mendel/Corbis; 32 Julia Waterlow; Eye Ubiquitous/Corbis; 33 Kerstin Geier; Gallo
Images/Corbis; 36 Mast Irham/epa/Corbis; 37 Jim Sugar/Corbis; 38 Naturfoto Honal/
Corbis; 40 Copyright SkySails; 43 Ben Shepard copyright Project Web
Front cover Penny Tweedie/Corbis

Printed in China

Franklin Watts is a division of Hachette Children's Books,
an Hachette Livre UK company.
www.hachettelivre.co.uk

The Coriolis effect

In 1835 the French scientist Gustave Gaspard Coriolis (1792-1843) described the effect that was later named after him. Coriolis noticed that the Earth's rotation affects the motion of anything travelling across the face of the globe - including moving air. Winds moving away from the equator curve to the east. Those moving towards the equator curve west.

(because its circumference is smaller). In a third area near the poles, cool air reaches faster-spinning areas and forms easterly winds.

Can we rely on the wind?

In general terms, we can certainly rely on the wind continuing to blow. The global pattern of wind circulation is caused by energy from the Sun, which experts say will keep shining steadily for another five billion years! There is no reason to believe that the Earth will not continue to spin, adding to the creation of wind through the Coriolis effect. However, local winds in any one spot on Earth can vary and this has led some critics to claim that wind power is unreliable. Local research gives planners a great deal of information about average wind conditions, and helps them plan accordingly.

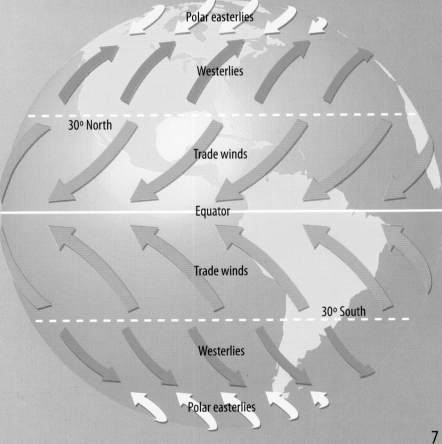

Polar easterlies

Westerlies

30º North

Trade winds

Equator

Trade winds

30º South

Westerlies

Polar easterlies

The global pattern of wind circulation is caused by temperature differences and the Earth's rotation. Further away from the equator, the moving air is cooler.

7

Wind strength

We measure the strength of the wind according to the speed of the moving air. Wind speed is usually given in kilometres (or miles) per hour or metres per second. Meteorologists keep records of wind speed, along with other data, so energy specialists have information to work with when looking at the position of turbines.

The two most important factors are the average wind speed and wind distribution. These tell us how windy a particular place is. The distribution explains variations in the general pattern of wind speed in one place. This is called the Weibull distribution. It is named after Swedish scientist Wallodi Weibull (1887-1979), who first described it. The diagram opposite shows a good example. The average wind speed in this place was worked out from measurements taken over

The winds off the sea in Morecambe Bay, in north-west England, have bent these trees into dramatic shapes.

Useful wind

Because of the design of spinning blades, very low and very high wind speeds cannot generate power. Very strong winds turn the blades too fast, making the turbine structure dangerous, so modern windmills have special control and braking systems (see page 21). Turbines are designed to start and stop turning at specific wind speeds. These usually vary between about 3 and 25 m/s (levels 2-9 on the Beaufort scale). The maximum useful wind speed is generally about 15 m/s (Beaufort 7).

a year. These were plotted on a graph, which shows that the median (or middle value) is 6.6 metres per second (m/s). The graph also shows that the wind speed was often half that level, but rarely double that amount.

Beaufort scale

Weather forecasts today still give wind speeds according to a scale developed in 1805 by Francis Beaufort (1774-1857), who was an officer in the British Royal Navy.

Beaufort number	Description	km/h	m/s
0	Calm	-1	-0.3
1	Light air	1-5	0.3-1.5
2	Light breeze	6-11	1.6-3.2
3	Gentle breeze	12-19	3.3-5.5
4	Moderate breeze	20-28	5.6-7.9
5	Fresh breeze	29-38	8.0-10.6
6	Strong breeze	39-49	10.7-13.6
7	Moderate gale	50-61	13.7-17.0
8	Fresh gale	62-74	17.1-21.0
9	Strong gale	75-88	21.1-24.5
10	Whole gale	89-102	24.6-28.0
11	Storm	103-118	28.1-33.0
12	Hurricane	119+	33.1+

WEIBULL DISTRIBUTION OF WIND SPEED

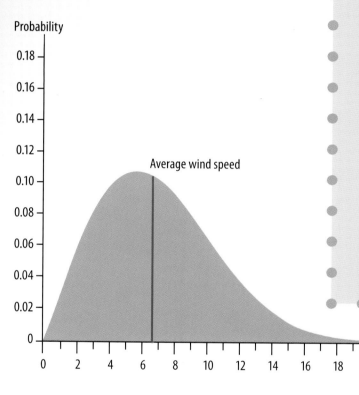

Probability / Average wind speed / metres per second

How do we measure wind speed?

Today, wind speed is usually measured with a device called an anemometer (from the Greek word *anemos*, meaning wind). The first wind meter was invented in Italy around 1450 and was based on a spinning disc. In 1846, an Irish physicist named Thomas Robinson (1792-1882) invented a four-cup anemometer. This device had cups which caught wind from any direction and turned. The wind speed was measured by the number of turns the cups made in a given period and was registered on a set of dials. Today, most anemometers have three cups, and there are also smaller, hand-held versions with built-in rotating propellers. The highest wind speeds of all – caused by tornadoes – are measured by a system called Doppler radar. In 1999, this system measured a world-record wind speed of 512 km/h in a tornado that devastated Oklahoma City, USA.

From sailing ships to windmills

Humans probably first harnessed the power of the wind when they started using sails to move boats across water. Early rafts may have had sails attached, but archaeological evidence for this is difficult to find. The earliest historical information records sailing boats more than 5000 years ago in ancient Egypt.

Against the current

Ancient Egyptians made their first boats from bundles of papyrus reeds lashed together. By 3000 BC these boats had oars and a long, narrow sail. The centre of Egyptian society was the River Nile, which formed the main highway of the empire, and the Egyptians used boats to fish, hunt and transport grain and cattle. Sailors travelled downstream towards the Mediterranean Sea on the strong Nile current. They used wind power to travel back upstream and return south to Thebes, Aswan and beyond.

Trading ships

During the Egyptian Old Kingdom (2686-2181 BC), shipbuilders made stronger vessels of wooden planks. These sturdy ships were able to venture further from land, and Egyptian sailors first made their way to the

Traditional Egyptian boats called feluccas still sail on the Nile today. They remind us that sailors have used the power of the wind since ancient times.

Mediterranean island of Crete (the home of the Minoan civilization). They also sailed to Phoenicia (modern Syria, Lebanon and Israel), where they acquired the famous trees called cedars of Lebanon. By the time of the Middle Kingdom (2055-1650 BC) there was regular sea trade between the two empires. The Egyptians then looked towards the lands of East Africa and the Indian Ocean. They carried boats in pieces across the eastern desert to the Red Sea, where they put them together again. According to the ancient Greek historian Herodotus, around 600 BC an Egyptian trading fleet left a Red Sea port and returned to Egypt more than two years later via the Mediterranean.

Powering across the oceans

Sailing ships were used by all early explorers and adventurers. Between the ninth and twelfth centuries, Scandinavian Vikings made the strongest, fastest ships. On the open sea, their longships were powered by a single square sail. This was made of tough woollen cloth strengthened by strips of leather. In the tenth century, a Norwegian Viking named Erik the Red sailed across the Atlantic Ocean to Greenland. His son, Leif Eriksson, travelled even further, to the coast of North America, around the year 1000 – nearly 500 years before the transatlantic voyages of Christopher Columbus.

This ninth-century Viking ship was powered by oars and a large square sail.

Speeding with the wind

Today, we still use fast sailing ships for sport and recreation. In the nineteenth century, everything was different. Clippers were the fastest ships in the world before the days of aeroplanes, even after the first successful steamship was launched in 1807. They may have gained their name from their sharp bows, fast 'clipping' speed, or because they clipped days off usual sailing times. Clippers had light wooden hulls and up to six rows of sails on at least three masts. They were used to speed tea from China to Europe and wool from Australia, and carried people around the Americas during the California gold rush. Clippers probably reached speeds of up to 22 knots (41 km/h), the same as a fast racing yacht today.

This old post mill stands on the Swedish island of Öland. There are hundreds of windmills on the island, and some date back to the seventeenth century.

Wind-powered wheels

The first person known to have used a wind-powered wheel was a Greek scientist and inventor called Hero. He lived in the Roman-controlled Egyptian city of Alexandria around AD 10-70. Hero invented an organ played by the wind. The wind turned the sails of a wheel, pushing a piston pump that forced air through the organ pipes.

By the seventh century, the first windmills were being constructed in Persia (modern-day Iran). These ground (or milled) grain such as wheat. The mill wheels and sails were parallel to the ground and turned on a vertical shaft that came out of a square tower. The design was probably based on early waterwheels, which had been known for many centuries. As the wind caught the sails and turned the horizontal wheel, the attached shaft turned a pair of stones. Grain poured between the stones was ground into flour.

Spreading technology

The new technology spread east in the 1220s, when the forces of the great Mongol conqueror Genghis Khan captured Persian millwrights and took them to China. By that time, windmills had also spread to Europe, possibly introduced by Crusaders returning from

Does the old technology still work?

The technology still works, but millers find that wind is less efficient and powerful than other sources of energy. James Watt (1736-1819) built the first steam-powered flour mill in 1780, and in the twentieth century steam was overtaken by electricity. Today, flour is usually milled between electrically powered steel rollers rather than stones. Nevertheless, some old windmills have been renovated and still produce stoneground flour. An example is Outwood post mill, in Surrey, England, which was built in 1665 and is the oldest working windmill in the UK.

the wars in the Middle East. By the late twelfth century, European millwrights had begun to set their wind-powered wheels in the vertical position that we see today. They found their windmills were more powerful when the wheel turned on a horizontal shaft. Windmills were especially popular in parts of Europe where there were few fast-flowing streams to drive watermills.

Post mills

Early European windmills had a box-like wooden body that contained the millstones and other machinery, such as gears. The box was mounted on a large wooden post attached to the horizontal windshaft (or axle). The vertical sails were outside the box, attached to the windshaft. The important thing about the post mill was that the whole structure could be turned around to face and catch the wind, whichever direction it was blowing from. Workers pushed the post mill around when the wind changed.

Turning towers

The next windmill development took place in the fifteenth century, when all the machinery was put inside a fixed tower, with a revolving cap on top. The sails were attached to the cap, so that they could more easily turn to face the wind. Wooden versions were called smock mills, and the sturdier stone or brick kinds are known as tower mills. From that time, tower mills became common throughout Europe.

This diagram of a tower mill shows the working parts, stores and accommodation. Grain was poured on to the millstones to make meal (coarse flour).

cap

windshaft

brake

brake wheel

sail

wallower

grain hopper

spur wheel

millstone

meal floor

grain store

bedroom

living room

WIND POWER

Windshaft, gears and cogs

Most windmills have four sails which drive a windshaft. A toothed cogwheel attached to the windshaft turns another wheel linked to a vertical main shaft. This shaft turns grooved millstones, and grain is poured into holes in the stones to be ground into flour. The action of the linked cogwheels means that the millstones turn about five times faster than the wind-driven sails.

Draining and raising water

The Netherlands is famous for windmills, but many of them are not mills at all. They should really be called wind pumps, because they are used to move water. Dutch people have been using wind power to drain their land since the fifteenth century. The Netherlands is very low-lying, and almost half its land is below sea level. Much of this land has been reclaimed from the sea by pumping water into drainage channels and then building banks and dykes around areas of land called polders. The pumps used the same system as mills, turning a scoop wheel instead of millstones. The turning wheel scooped up water and poured it into a higher-level ditch or basin. Engineers often built several wind pumps in a row, so that water could be raised slightly higher by each one. In the nineteenth century there were 9000 windmills and wind pumps in the Netherlands, but many were replaced by steam engines.

A series of three wind pumps reclaims land by moving water from the polder to a drainage channel. This channel takes the water back to the sea.

lower pump

middle pump

upper pump

dyke

scoop wheel

polder water   lower basin   intermediate basin   waterway across dyke   drainage channel

Pumping up

In southern Europe, which has a warm Mediterranean climate, wind pumps were traditionally used to bring water to the surface from deep underground. On the Greek island of Crete there were once 10,000 white-sailed pumps. Today, most have been replaced by electric and diesel-driven engines.

During the last two centuries, small wind pumps have been used in the United States. The turning shaft drives a pump rod that operates a piston to pump water to the surface. A relatively small wind-powered pump with rotors ten metres in diameter can pump about 200 litres of water a minute from a depth of 30 metres. The water is stored in a tank and used to irrigate crops or as drinking water.

This wind pump provides water for cattle on a farm in Nebraska, USA.

Wind-powered pumps today

Wind pumps are still used all over the world, especially in dry areas. Concerns about the environment and a desire to use renewable sources of energy have increased interest in this traditional technology. There are still some wind-powered pumps in the United States and Australia, and manufacturers are promoting their environmental advantages. Wind pumps are particularly useful in the arid regions of Africa, such as Kenya, Namibia and South Africa, where they provide water for villagers and livestock.

15

Sawmill

In 1592 the Dutch millwright Cornelis Corneliszoon (1550-1607) invented a wind-driven sawmill. He fixed the main shaft of the mill to saw blades, which moved up and down. The blades cut lengths of timber as they passed through — up to 30 times faster than men could. The mill was mounted on a raft, so that it could be turned into the wind.

Wind-powered electricity

Charles Brush (1849-1929) was an American inventor best known for his arc lamp, which was an important form of electric lighting before the invention of the incandescent light bulb. In 1879 Brush devised an electric lighting system for a public square in Cleveland, Ohio. Soon Brush's arc lamps were lighting streets in Boston, New York and San Francisco, making their inventor rich. In 1888 Brush decided to try a new system for generating electricity. He had been using a horse-drawn treadmill to power a dynamo, or simple generator, but then he replaced horse power with the wind. Brush built a large wind-wheel in the garden of his Cleveland mansion. The wheel drove a dynamo that charged 408 batteries in the basement of the mansion, which in turn lit 350 incandescent lights and some of his own arc lamps.

Brush's wind-dynamo facts and figures

Tower height: 18 m

Tower weight: 36 tonnes

Wheel diameter: 17 m

Number of wooden wheel blades: 144

Windshaft length: 6 m

Fantail length: 18 m

Top wheel speed: 10 revolutions per minute (rpm)

Electricity production: 12 kilowatts (kW)

Increasing efficiency

In 1890 Poul La Cour (1846-1908), a Danish high-school teacher, scientist and inventor, began testing ways of using wind-wheels to generate electricity. La Cour was particularly interested in supplying electric power – which all scientists saw as the future – to small villages in

Poul La Cour's early wind turbine, which was built along the lines of a traditional windmill. Later versions had an iron framework and four sails.

the countryside. He built a wind turbine that was based on traditional windmills, with six sails mounted on a wooden tower. The wheels were attached to turbine buildings, and La Cour found that turbines which turned faster and had fewer rotor blades were more efficient for producing electricity. Denmark has remained one of the world's largest producers of wind-produced energy.

Scientific progress over a century

Charles Brush and Poul La Cour were pioneers in the field of wind-generated electricity. La Cour founded the Society of Wind Electricians in Denmark in 1903, and the following year he published the world's first journal on the subject of wind-generated electricity. Some environmentalists believe that more research could lead to the development of more effective technology. The World Wind Energy Association (WWEA) was founded in 2001, with headquarters in Bonn, Germany. The association holds an annual global conference in a different part of the world each year. Since 2007, the WWEA has been represented on the Economic and Social Council of the United Nations. Perhaps we should put even more effort into scientific progress?

Turbines today

The most important way we use wind power today is in generating electricity. Today's wind turbines have an electric generator in their housing, unlike those developed at the end of the nineteenth century. They are sometimes called aerogenerators (*aero* meaning air or wind).

Electricity generation began during the nineteenth century. In 1831 the British scientist Michael Faraday (1791-1867) discovered that he could create electricity by moving a magnet through a coil of copper wire. This process, called electromagnetic induction, led to the invention of the electric generator, which works by changing mechanical energy into electrical energy. The power of moving air provides the mechanical energy for wind turbines by turning the rotor blades. The blades are connected to a shaft, which is also attached to a generator. Inside the generator, the shaft makes magnets spin inside wire coils to produce electricity.

The rotor

The rotor is the assembly of blades that is turned by the wind. The blades are made of strong polyester plastic reinforced with glass fibre or carbon fibre and attached to a steel hub. The blades look like an aeroplane wing, or aerofoil. The upper side facing the wind is curved and the lower side is flat. This creates greater air pressure on the lower side, giving lift and forcing the blade forwards so the hub rotates. Large turbines have an automatic controlling device to change the pitch (or angle) of the blades. If the wind is too strong and the blades are moving too fast, the blade is turned slightly to reduce the lift and speed.

Horizontal axis turbines

There are two basic types of wind turbine: horizontal axis and vertical axis versions, called HAWTs and VAWTs (horizontal or vertical axis wind turbines). The most common kind today is the three-blade HAWT (see right). This has proved to be the most efficient for power generation by large wind turbines with a rotor diameter of 40-90 metres. The three blades make the rotation smoother and make the turbine seem less visually intrusive than two, four or more blades.

A wind turbine nacelle (or pod) cut away to show the workings inside. The yaw drive at the top of the tower turns the turbine so it faces into the wind.

Are wind turbines noisy?

Most experts agree that modern turbines produce less mechanical noise than early versions, although the flow of air over the blades still makes a whooshing noise. The UK Sustainable Development Commission says: 'Turbine design has improved substantially as the technology has advanced, with noise from the moving parts progressively reduced. The public's concern about noise from turbines is often related to perceptions rather than actual experience. Detailed studies have shown that the very low levels of low frequency noise from wind turbines will not normally cause adverse health effects.' The commission says the sound from a turbine is generally about 90-100 dB (similar to a pneumatic drill at seven metres), or 50-60 dB at a distance of 40 metres (similar to a busy office) and 25-35 dB at 500 metres (similar to a quiet room). In other words, the noise is only a problem if you are very close to a turbine.

wind direction

1. Blade
2. Pitch
3. Hub
4. Nacelle
5. Low-speed shaft
6. Brake
7. High-speed shaft
8. Gear
9. Generator
10. Anemometer
11. Wind vane
12. Yaw drive
13. Tower

WIND POWER

Tower and pod

Towers are usually made of steel or concrete, and the tallest reach well over 100 metres. One of the latest German wind turbines is 135 metres high at the hub and has a rotor diameter of 126 metres. Manufacturers prefabricate the towers in three or four parts and use cranes to assemble and erect them at the site.

Taller towers have less turbulence from ground features and so catch the wind better. At the top of the tower is the streamlined nacelle (or pod), which turns according to the wind direction. A wind vane at the back of the pod sends signals to an onboard computer, which calculates the best direction and moves the pod with an electric yaw motor.

Gearing up

Inside the pod, the turning shaft is connected to a gearbox. This has a set of gears (or toothed wheels), which increase the spinning speed. The gearbox converts the energy from the rotor. When the rotor is

Opposite: towers are hollow, so that engineers can climb a ladder inside to check and service working parts.

Assembly workers are dwarfed by the giant nacelle of this German wind turbine. One of the three rotor blades has been installed on the hub, at a height of 124 metres.

Withstanding the weather

Manufacturers have to allow for extreme weather conditions when designing and building wind turbines. The tower has to withstand very strong forces and is built on sturdy foundations. Some manufacturers offer what they call 'hurricane-resistant' towers. Most turbines also have automatic braking systems, which slow the speed of the shaft if it is turning dangerously fast. They often have a mechanical disc brake behind the hub, which backs up the actions of the pitched blades and can be used as a parking brake when the turbine is out of action.

To counteract lightning strikes during thunderstorms, turbines have special receptors which conduct electricity to the ground. These include aluminium blade tips, metal discs along the blades and conductors along the pod and tower. The lightning is kept away from sensitive parts of the turbine that might be damaged. In case of fire, turbines also have automatic extinguishers. Many turbines have heating and cooling systems for the working parts, which are especially useful in extreme climates.

turning at 10-22 rpm, it converts that to about 1500 rpm, so the generator shaft is turned much more quickly and produces electricity more effectively.

Do wind turbines work most of the time?

Turbines rely on wind conditions. Opponents to wind power say that turbines are inefficient and work only 30 per cent of the time. In fact, industry experts claim that is the overall percentage of electricity they produce compared with the maximum electricity they could generate in theory. Modern wind turbines produce electricity 70-85 per cent of the time, but at different rates depending on wind speed. Over the course of a year, they therefore generate between 25 and 40 per cent of their possible maximum output (with usually more in winter than summer). This compares with biomass plants at 60-90 per cent, combined cycle gas turbine (CCGT) plants at 70-85 per cent, coal-fired and nuclear plants at 65-85 per cent, and hydropower at 25-50 per cent.

Vertical axis turbines

Vertical axis wind turbines (VAWTs) have a windshaft or main axle which stands upright from the ground (like the tower of a HAWT). The turbine blades do not swivel to face the wind, as they are pushed by winds from any direction. This design allows the generator to be close to the ground, which makes it easier to reach for servicing and repairs. On the other hand, ground winds tend to be more turbulent than high-level winds.

Different designs

In 1931 the French aeronautical engineer Georges Darrieus (1888-1979) patented his vertical turbine. It was a distinctive shape, with up to four curved blades attached to a vertical shaft, and was soon known as the eggbeater. This is the only VAWT that has been made commercially in any volume, but it does have problems. One is that it does not perform well in high winds and has to be held firmly in place with steel cables or an outer structure. Another is that the eggbeater is difficult to start in normal winds, so an electric motor has to kick-start its rotation.

Georges Darrieus' turbine patent covered almost any arrangement of vertical aerofoil blades. This made things difficult for other engineers. One later design was the giromill (or H-bar or cross-arm design), which has straight vertical blades attached to a central tower with horizontal supports. The giromill design is

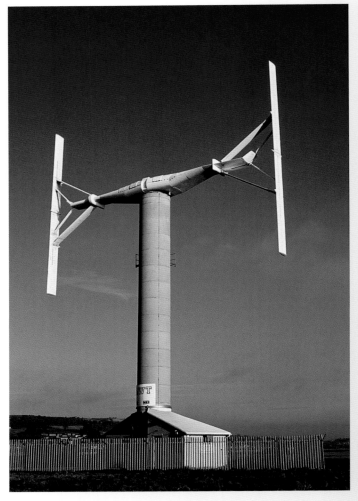

This vertical axis turbine can produce 130 kW of electricity. The E-112 shown on page 20 can generate 6 MW, which is 46 times more.

How efficient?

Experts have found that vertical turbines are generally not as efficient as horizontal turbines. Most VAWTs produce energy at only half the efficiency of HAWTs. This is mainly because of the additional drag that they are exposed to as their blades turn back into the wind on the way back to their starting point.

Investing in wind power

Engineers such as Georges Darrieus were inventing new turbines 80 years ago, and inventors are still working on innovative designs. Some environmental groups think we should invest much more money in turbine research and development, in the hope that engineers may be able to increase their efficiency. Others feel that governments should be investing more in wind power so that the initial costs can be subsidized and companies are encouraged to develop new systems. Large wind turbines are expensive to develop and build, but once they are running, the power needed to run them — the wind — is free. Some countries have what is called a feed-in tariff. This is the price per unit of electricity that a national or regional energy supplier pays for electricity from renewable sources (including wind) from private generators. The government regulates the tariff (or price), and this helps new energy-generating companies to become established so they can compete with older suppliers, who mainly burn fossil fuels.

simpler to build than the eggbeater, but the structure is heavier and the blades need to be much stronger. A similar version is called a cycloturbine.

This series of Darrieus eggbeater turbines stretches across a hillside in California, USA.

Onshore and offshore

Individual wind turbines do not produce enormous amounts of electricity compared with power stations fired by fossil fuels. A large aerogenerator may produce just one megawatt (MW) of power, though the biggest are six or seven times more powerful. If you compare this with a large coal-fired power station, which can produce 5000 MW, it is easy to see why energy companies put wind turbines together in big groups.

Groups called wind farms (or sometimes wind parks) form small power plants. They are often sited on land, but there is increasing interest in offshore wind farms.

The World Wind Energy Association says that wind is used to generate electricity in more than 70 countries. The amount of electricity produced has been growing by more than 25 per cent a year in recent times. In 2007, wind generated 1.3 per cent of the electricity used in the world and provided electricity for more than 25 million

PRODUCTION OF WIND POWER (MW)
AND PERCENTAGE OF WORLD OUTPUT (%)

- GERMANY 22,247 (23.7%)
- USA 16,819 (17.9%)
- SPAIN 15,145 (16.1%)
- INDIA 7,850 (8.4%)
- CHINA 5,899 (6.3%)
- DENMARK 3,125 (3.3%)
- ITALY 2,726 (2.9%)
- FRANCE 2,455 (2.6%)
- UK 2,389 (2.5%)
- PORTUGAL 2,130 (2.3%)

This wind farm has been built on top of a hill.
This is a good location for wind power.

homes. In some countries, wind-generated electricity adds up to more than 40 per cent. As the table opposite shows, the four leading wind-energy countries together make up two thirds of world production.

Finding the right location

Engineers look for exactly the right site for wind farms. They study local winds in likely locations for many months and make wind maps for energy companies to study. Experts have found that long narrow hilltops are good sites. They add height so that there is more wind, and it accelerates over the top of the hill, adding wind speed to generate more energy.

What is a watt?

A watt (W) is a unit of power which measures the rate of producing or using energy. The term was named after the Scottish engineer James Watt (1736-1819), who developed an improved steam engine. Watt himself measured his engine's performance in horsepower (hp). One horsepower equals 746 watts. Today, watts are generally used to measure electric power.

1 kilowatt (kW) = 1 thousand watts
1 megawatt (MW) = 1 million watts
1 gigawatt (GW) = 1 thousand million watts

What are the advantages of wind power?

The main advantage is the fact that wind is a simple form of renewable energy (see page 34). What else could you add? The Global Wind Energy Council lists the 12 advantages below.

'Wind power...

- is clean, free and indigenous;
- combats climate change;
- reduces air pollution;
- provides energy security;
- diversifies energy supply;
- eliminates imported fuels;
- prevents conflict over natural resources;
- improves rural electrification and reduces poverty;
- creates jobs, regional growth and innovation;
- hedges price volatility of fossil fuels;
- delivers power on a large scale;
- is modular and quick to install.'

Winds are usually stronger near the coast, so it is not surprising that many wind farms are located at so-called nearshore sites. These are either on land within three kilometres of the coast or at sea within ten kilometres of the coast. In this 13-kilometre wide zone wind farms can use both onshore and offshore winds.

Largest farm

The world's largest wind farm is more than 500 kilometres from the nearest coast. Horse Hollow Wind Energy Center covers a large area of land near Abilene, Texas, where the closest sea is the Gulf of Mexico. The Center was built in 2005-06 and produces enough electricity to power about 220,000 homes. When the wind farm opened, some local people complained about the appearance of the turbines and the noise they created. The case went to court, but a judge and jury decided that the wind farm was not a nuisance and did not invade the locals' privacy.

Horse Hollow Center facts and figures

Total area: 240 sq km

Number of turbines: 421

Turbine height: 80 m

Cut-off wind speed: 90 km/h (Beaufort 10)

Total electricity production: 735 MW

Farming ocean winds

The surface of the ocean is much smoother than land, so the average wind speed over open water is usually much higher. This means that offshore wind farms can be more efficient and powerful than onshore parks. Turbines are easiest to build in shallow waters, because their foundations have to be built on the seabed. Countries with long coastlines and shallow continental shelves – such as Denmark and the UK – offer many good locations for offshore wind farms.

This row of nearshore turbines lies just off the coast of Denmark.

Success at sea

The Horns Rev wind farm, 14 kilometres off the Danish coast in the North Sea, was built in 2002 and is a success. The farm has 80 turbines, each 70 metres tall, which cover a sea area of about 20 sq km. The turbines are set 560 metres apart in shallow water up to a maximum of 38 metres deep. The farm's operators claim that this offshore farm produces more than twice as much electricity as a similar onshore wind farm.

Can turbines be close together?

They can be fairly close together. However, each wind turbine creates turbulence, spoiling the powerful flow of air to other turbines by creating gusts. Engineers work out exactly how to position a series of turbines. They are often spaced three to five rotor diameters apart at right angles to the direction of the prevailing wind. If there is another row of turbines behind, they are positioned between five and ten rotor diameters away. The precise positioning can make a huge difference to the overall efficiency of a wind farm.

WIND POWER

The London Array wind farm could be completed by 2010. The turbines will stand in water up to 23 metres deep and will be up to 100 metres tall. Generated electricity will be fed into the British national grid at Cleve Hill.

Biggest in the world...

At the end of 2006, approval was given for the construction of the world's largest offshore wind farm – London Array (an array is a very large group). It will be built on and between two sandbanks more than 20 kilometres off the Kent and Essex coasts, in the outer Thames estuary. It will take four years to build and will produce enough electricity to power about 750,000 homes. The government hopes that the array will produce 10 per cent of its renewable energy target when it comes into operation.

London Array facts and figures

Total area: 245 sq km

Number of turbines: 341

Turbine height: 100 m

Cut-off wind speed: 90 km/h (Beaufort 10)

Total electricity production: up to 1 GW

A supergrid under the sea

The electricity generated by wind turbines is fed into cables that join the main electricity network at the nearest available point. Offshore wind farm cables run beneath the surface of the sea, usually on the seabed. In Europe, Irish and Swiss engineers are working on a project called a subsea supergrid. The idea is to connect up lots of small electricity networks from offshore wind farms along Europe's coastline. When the wind blows over a farm on the supergrid, its cables will carry

A 52-metre long rotor blade is carefully checked at a factory in Denmark. It has been made in one piece, and its curved shape must be exactly right.

electricity to where it is needed most. If the wind is not blowing over the North Sea, it is likely to be doing so in the Baltic or Irish Sea. The aim of the supergrid is to make wind power more accessible and reliable, at the same time linking separate countries so that they can trade energy.

Onshore or offshore?

This is a difficult question. Offshore turbines cause some problems for shipping, but energy companies and environmentalists are generally in favour of them. One proposed offshore project is in Nantucket Sound, a large area of shallow water off the coast of Massachusetts, USA. The environmental group Greenpeace says: 'This wind farm project will provide 74 per cent of Cape Cod's energy needs with clean and safe wind power. It could dramatically reduce the need for the Cape's current oil and gas burning power plant, which caused a major oil spill in Buzzard's Bay in 2003... Greenpeace has 30 years history defending the world's oceans. We would... oppose this proposal if we felt that it posed long-term threats to the marine ecosystem of Nantucket Sound. We agree Nantucket Sound is a beautiful place that is heavily used by tourists, locals, part-time residents, fisherpeople, and commercial interests. We support offshore wind in Nantucket Sound because we see it as an important step in our fight for renewable energy solutions to global warming.'

Small-scale turbines

Small-scale wind power can supply individual homes, businesses or small communities. In the industrialized world, this is a popular way for environmentally conscious people to produce their own electricity. One of the most successful markets for 'small wind' is the United States. The American Wind Energy Association claims that energy generated by small turbines (up to 100 kW capacity) is growing by 18-20 per cent every year.

Encouraging wind power

Wind systems are expensive to install individually, and the initial cost may take more than five years to pay off in reduced electricity bills for a homeowner. In many countries the government offers grants towards the cost of installing a small turbine. Many governments also allow homeowners to sell surplus electricity created by the turbine to the national grid. This seems fair and increases the overall percentage of electricity produced from renewable sources.

Micro turbines

Some very small (or micro) turbines supply energy for battery-charging systems, and these are often used on boats and on some homes. For houses, there are two kinds of turbine. One is mast-mounted and stands on the

Ecovillages for the future?

Ecovillages are communities in which people try to live in a way that does as little harm as possible to the natural environment. Ecovillagers do all they can to keep their soil, water and air clean, and they prefer to use renewable energy. Many rely on the wind (as well as solar power) for electricity, because they consider these to be the most environmentally friendly methods. These examples of modern living could encourage others to follow the trend.

People living in an ecovillage in Scotland use electricity supplied by a wind turbine.

ground near the building. The other is the much cheaper roof-mounted turbine, which is often attached to a chimney. People considering their own wind system need to check the average wind speed and direction where they live and to get expert advice before they install a system.

Problems with small wind

Some reports have found that rooftop turbines produce only about a quarter of an average household's electricity needs, which has disappointed some householders. Small turbines do not always work well in urban areas, where wind often blows around in squally gusts. Some have found that roof-mounted turbines cause structural damage to chimneys and gable ends. Turbulence also puts great stress on the turbines and shortens their life, though most experts say that they should last up to 20 years. People may notice vibration from the turbine, and they may be a bit noisy. As with other technologies, increased use and technical developments may eradicate these problems and make home installation more attractive in the near future.

WIND POWER

Off-grid in China

China is a vast country with an enormous population (the world's largest) and fast-growing energy needs. Other countries supply China with renewable technology, including wind turbines, and by the end of 2005 China had 59 wind farms with 1854 turbines. The country was tenth in the world for wind-generated electricity. Two years later it was fifth (see page 24).

By 2020, the Chinese government plans to generate 30 gigawatts of wind power – five times more than in 2007. Much of this will come from small, off-grid schemes in remote communities. One of the most successful small-scale wind energy programmes is in the northern region of Inner Mongolia, where around 130,000 small turbines provide electricity for more than half a million people.

Practical action in Sri Lanka

More than two thirds of Sri Lankans live in rural areas far from the electricity grid. The charity Practical Action has been helping by supplying them with small wind turbines, which people use to recharge the car batteries that power their homes.

Watering game reserves

In Africa, many game reserves have small wind pumps to keep waterholes filled. The pumps are similar to those still used on American farms (see page 15). A good example of wind turbine use is in Etosha National Park, in Namibia, which is one of southern Africa's most important game reserves.

A wind turbine provides power for a small community in Inner Mongolia province, China.

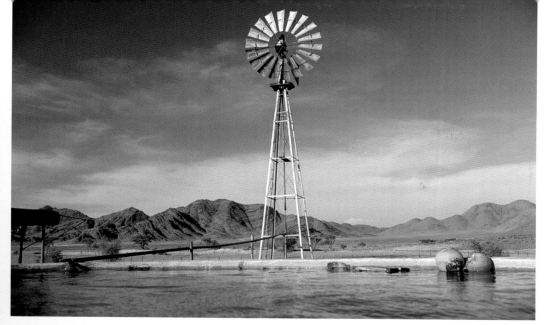

One of the wind pumps that helps to water the dry regions of Namibia.

Covering an area of 22,270 sq km, Etosha (meaning great white place and named after a dried-up lake) was made a national park in 1907. Today it is home to 114 species of mammals, 110 species of reptiles and 340 of birds. Visitors come to see elephants, giraffes, rhinos and lions. Without the wind's help in bringing water to the surface, the animals would struggle to survive in this very dry environment.

Windy Patagonia

Patagonia is a dry, windswept plateau in southern Argentina. It makes up more than a quarter of Argentina but is home to less than three per cent of the country's people. Patagonia has many remote villages and small isolated communities, and since the beginning of the twenty-first century small wind-power projects have brought them electricity. The region has strong, constant winds, usually blowing at about 11 m/s (a strong breeze on the Beaufort scale), so people know they can rely on the technology. Many houses are powered by a three-blade, 12-metre high turbine with 600-watt power.

Do tourists hate wind turbines?

Tourism is very important to many poorer countries, and it has been suggested that turbines discourage tourists. There is no real evidence to back this up, however. In Africa, wind pumps positively encourage tourism by ensuring that animals have water to drink (see above). In Denmark, where wind power is very popular, many tour companies run boat trips taking foreign visitors to see the 20 offshore wind turbines at Middelgrunden, just outside Copenhagen harbour. The turbines, which provide four per cent of the city's electricity, have become a new landmark for tourists. In the United States, the wind farm at Searsburg, Vermont, runs successful educational tours. Their popularity has influenced locals. When the turbines were put up, two thirds of local people supported them. After seeing their success, 83 per cent of people said they felt positive about them.

Caring for the environment

One of the greatest benefits of wind power is that it is renewable, so it does not harm the environment. Wind power compares favourably with non-renewable energy sources (fossil fuels and nuclear power) and environmentalists believe that it is green and clean. Opponents claim that there are disadvantages such as noise, but most people seem to feel positive about it.

The Earth's atmosphere prevents some of the Sun's rays from reaching Earth. The gases in the atmosphere also stop some heat escaping from Earth, just as glass traps warmth inside a greenhouse. We are adding to this natural greenhouse effect by emitting so many waste gases from power plants, factories and cars. Many of these greenhouse gases – especially carbon dioxide – are produced when we burn coal, oil or gas to release energy. Experts have discovered that in this way humans are making natural climate change more extreme. The way we use energy is adding to global warming, so that land, sea and air

The greenhouse effect traps some heat inside the atmosphere near the Earth's surface. The effect is increased by carbon dioxide and other gases.

reflected

absorbed

edge of atmosphere

absorbed by atmosphere and Earth

radiation absorbed by greenhouse gases

greenhouse gases and fossil fuels

deforestation

oil and petrol engines

CFCs

Comparing sources

Wind scores on four important counts against fossil fuels and nuclear power. As well as releasing greenhouse gases, fossil fuels pollute the atmosphere. Mining causes problems (including mining uranium for nuclear power stations), and there is no safe way to deal with nuclear waste.

Environmental problems	Wind	Nuclear	Natural gas/oil	Coal
Global warming pollution	no	no	yes	yes
Air pollution	no	no	yes	yes
Mining/extraction	no	yes	yes	yes
Disposal of waste	no	yes	no	yes

temperatures are gradually increasing. Using renewable energy sources, such as wind, can help reduce the increase in temperature which causes global warming.

Reducing carbon dioxide emissions

Carbon dioxide (CO_2) is the most important (or worst) greenhouse gas emitted by other power sources. According to the American Wind Energy Association (AWEA), a single 1-MW wind turbine cuts the emission of CO_2 per year by more than 1600 tonnes compared with the normal US fuel mix (including burning fossil fuels and nuclear power). At the same time, it also cuts emissions of sulphur dioxide by eight tonnes and of nitrogen oxide by nearly four tonnes. Power stations would need to burn more than 1300 tonnes of coal or more than 1400 barrels of oil to create the same amount of electricity.

How much energy to build a wind farm?

Opponents to wind power sometimes claim that building a wind farm requires more energy than its turbines will ever generate. Experts at the British Wind Energy Association disagree. They estimate that an average wind farm should generate the amount of energy used to build it within three to five months of coming into operation. This is better than coal-fired or nuclear power stations, which take about six months – and also create problems of pollution and waste.

Yes or no?

Adding together surveys made over a ten-year period in Britain, the following results emerged:
• 77 per cent of people are in favour of wind power;
• 14 per cent are neutral (don't know);
• 9 per cent are against.

Noisy or not?

One of the strongest general criticisms of wind turbines is that they are noisy. But experts say this is not the case, and long-term American studies back up this view. The AWEA says, 'The sound turbines produce is similar to a light whooshing or swishing sound, and much more quiet than other modern-day equipment. Even in rural or low-density areas, where there is little additional sound to mask that of the wind turbines, the sound of the blowing wind is often louder.'

Other potential problems

Some people have suggested that wind turbines produce infrasound (low-frequency noise), which cannot be heard by humans but can be felt as vibration. They are concerned that this might cause health problems for people living near wind farms, but research studies have shown that there is no cause for concern. Experts say that the infrasound levels are so low that they cannot cause any ill effects to people. However, in 2006 a family living 400 metres from the nearest turbine in a 17-unit wind farm in Nova Scotia, Canada, felt forced to move because they said low-frequency noise caused headaches and made them feel tired.

Shadow flicker

This term is used to describe shadows thrown by the rotating blades of a wind turbine. Some people who live near turbines have complained about this when the sun is low in the sky. But this would only be a problem for those living very close, and it could be investigated before construction.

Land use

One of the disadvantages of wind farms is that they take up a great deal of space, although individual or small groups of turbines require much less space. Supporters point out that the space needed for a wind

An Indonesian protester hands out plants on World Environment Day (5 June) in 2007. Environmentalists promote renewable energy to help all life on Earth.

The first turbines at this wind farm at Altamont Pass, California, were put up in 1981. They have since become a well-known landmark, but they have created problems too (see page 39).

farm compares favourably with the space taken up by large hydroelectric schemes with reservoirs or coal-fired power stations and the mines which supply them. Perhaps one of the biggest issues is that windswept coastlines and hills are popular with ramblers and nature-lovers.

'Not in my back yard!'

One of the problems with all electricity production is that people do not want to see unsightly technology from their living-room window. This is known as the NIMBY (Not In My Back Yard) attitude. People are happy to have wind farms or even other kinds of power stations, because they want a secure and plentiful supply of electricity, but they want them somewhere else.

Are wind turbines a blot on the landscape? Some people say so, but others see them as examples of modern, environmentally sound technology and find them attractive. Modern engineers

also do their best to design and site wind farms so that they do not look ugly. The environmental scientist James Lovelock writes: 'Wind energy, through crude and unsustainable industrial development, is already devastating some unusually beautiful countryside.' Greenpeace disagrees: 'Compared to mountain top removal from coal mining, oil extraction, nuclear power plants and other energy developers, wind farms are quite elegant.'

What do you think? Do you like the look of wind turbines? If you do, would you want them near your home?

Danger to birds...

Wind turbines are an obvious danger to birds. This is because wind farms are sited in areas where the wind blows steadily, and these locations tend to be on main routes for migratory birds. Also, studies have found that mice and other rodents use the bases of turbine towers as nesting places, which attracts birds of prey. As the bird circles above its prey, it is in great danger from rotating blades.

There has been a great deal of research in the United States, where it is estimated that more than 1000 birds of prey (including 100 golden eagles) may be killed each year by turbines. Nevertheless, the American Wind Energy Association (AWEA)

Research in the United States shows that turbine blades can kill golden eagles.

Wind energy and wildlife

The American Wind Energy Association claims that in terms of impact on wildlife, the wind energy industry has three main benefits. These are that it is:
• clean (environmentally friendly, protecting air quality and reducing the effects of global warming);
• compatible (with animals and humans, meaning that it does not harm them);
• committed (to ensuring minimal impact on nature and the environment).

points out that for every 10,000 birds killed by human activities, fewer than one is killed by a wind turbine. This single fatality compares with 5500 deaths caused by buildings, 1000 by domestic cats, 800 by electricity cables (some of which may be connected to wind farms, of course), 700 by vehicles and 700 by pesticides. In Britain, the Royal Society for the Protection of Birds says: 'The available evidence suggests that appropriately positioned wind farms do not pose a significant hazard for birds. However, evidence from the US and Spain confirms that poorly sited wind farms can cause severe problems for birds, through disturbance, habitat loss/damage or collision with turbines.'

What about offshore farms and fish?

Building offshore wind farms does affect marine wildlife, especially in spawning areas, and energy companies have been urged not to build during breeding periods. Turbine foundations on the seabed can act as artificial reefs and help to increase numbers of fish. However, the fishing industry is very unhappy about offshore wind farms, because they make it impossible for their boats to use these waters. Despite the conflicts, many wildlife conservationists believe that wind power should be encouraged because it combats the greatest threat of all — global warming.

... and bats

Studies have shown that bats are at risk from turbines during their autumn migration. In one year, 458 bats of seven different species were killed by 44 turbines at a West Virginia wind farm. More studies of bats are needed.

Problems at Altamont Pass

Research has been carried out at Altamont Pass wind farm, in California, which has about 5000 relatively small turbines sprawled over an area of 130 sq km. Recent studies suggest that several thousand birds may be killed there every year (between 1700 and 4700 birds), including golden eagles, red-tailed hawks, American kestrels and burrowing owls. The birds prey on the local ground squirrels. One survey found that the death rate was one bird for every five turbines per year. Environmentalists have forced the operators of the wind farm to close or move some turbines to reduce the number of birds killed. Newer turbines with a slower revolution speed also help cut the number of bird deaths.

What does the future hold?

Many people see wind power as an important source of energy, and this importance is certain to grow in future. Demand for electricity is likely to double over the next 25 years, and environmental groups will continue to put pressure on politicians and business leaders to encourage a greater use of renewable energy.

A report by the World Wind Energy Association (WWEA) states that our current use of wind power will grow by more than 25 per cent in the next few years. Many countries have set high targets for the percentage of energy they will generate from renewable sources by 2020, and wind power is likely to play a large part in helping governments reach those targets. By then, experts say that 25 million US homes, for example, will receive their energy from wind power.

Modern sailing ships

In recent years some modern ships have added sails to reduce the amount of diesel oil and other fuels they burn when sailing conditions are good. In 2008 a new type of wind-propelled cargo ship made its maiden voyage, from Germany across the Atlantic Ocean to Venezuela. This new ship has a 160 sq m kite-sail, similar

On its voyage across the Atlantic, the Beluga SkySails *used a fifth less fuel than usual by using wind power. This has caught the attention of other shipping companies.*

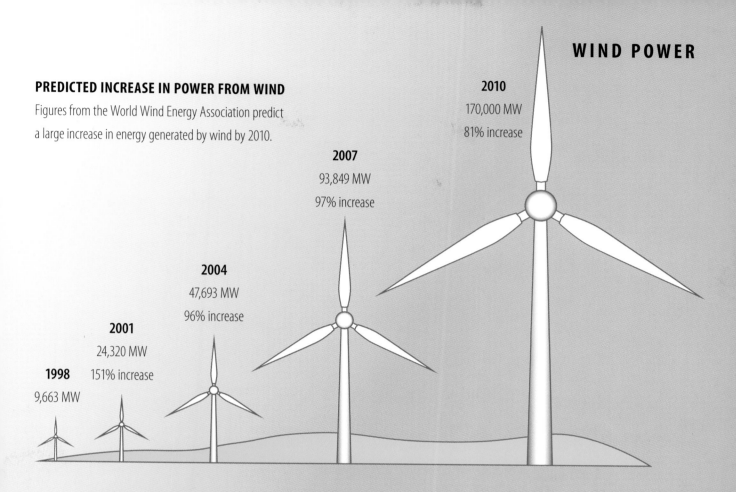

PREDICTED INCREASE IN POWER FROM WIND

Figures from the World Wind Energy Association predict
a large increase in energy generated by wind by 2010.

2010
170,000 MW
81% increase

2007
93,849 MW
97% increase

2004
47,693 MW
96% increase

2001
24,320 MW
151% increase

1998
9,663 MW

to the sail of a paraglider, which flies up to 300m
above the ship and allows high-level winds to tow
it along. The operators of the cargo ship believe
that the sail will save up to 35 per cent of the
ship's fuel. At the same time, it will lower
harmful carbon emissions.

Floating turbines

Researchers at the Massachusetts Institute of
Technology (MIT) and the US National Renewable
Energy Laboratory (NREL) have designed a wind
turbine that can be attached to a floating platform.
Steel cables secure the platform to a mooring on
the ocean floor. Tests have shown that the floating
platforms could survive hurricane winds. They
could operate in much deeper water than current
offshore turbines and further out to sea.

Counting the cost

Experts claim that the cost of wind-generated electricity
has fallen dramatically. Wind-power capacity has doubled
every three years, and prices have fallen each time by 15
per cent. Wind energy now competes with new coal and
nuclear power, even before environmental costs are taken
into account. Wind associations believe that the price of
wind-generated electricity will continue to fall. This depends
on investment and incentives (see page 23). The AWEA
says, 'There are no fuel costs, and in good locations the
"levelized" cost (the capital, the fuel, and the operations
and maintenance costs over the lifetime of the plant) of
wind energy can now be very competitive with that of other
energy sources.' Wind-power costs are fixed and predictable.

Dividing communities

The issue of large wind farms divides opinion all over the world. One recent example of the division of public attitudes is a proposal to build a 181-turbine wind farm on the Isle of Lewis, one of the Hebrides islands off the coast of western Scotland. The farm could produce 600 MW of electricity – enough to supply all the homes in Glasgow (Scotland's largest city). But it is an enormous project, requiring 137 large pylons to carry 31 km of overhead electricity cables, as well as the construction of 142 km of access roads. The project would create an enormous number of jobs and offer a huge income to the people of Lewis, and though some islanders are convinced of the advantages, many are not and continue to protest against the wind farm. There are likely to be more such debates in future.

Wind-powered buildings?

In future it may prove possible to include wind turbines in tall buildings. Architects and designers are planning to build large rotors into skyscrapers, or perhaps on top of the buildings. One of the problems is that buildings in cities cause turbulence, so that the wind streams are not constant or steady. Also, the proposed rotors take up a great deal of space. Nevertheless, it may be possible for a tall building to generate all its own electricity for residents or workers.

Airborne ideas

Scientists, engineers and inventors are all constantly working on new ideas for harvesting the wind. Many of them are concentrating on reaching high-speed winds higher up in the sky. Some scientists in the Netherlands are working on a system called a laddermill which has a loop of kites that rotate in the wind and turn a cable. An Australian professor is developing another system – called the gyromill – which would fly up to 4500 metres above the ground and send back electricity generated by spinning rotors.

This is how the wind-power system called a gyromill might look. It is just one of the exciting new developments in wind power being tested.

Will the wind debate continue?

People will continue to debate the merits of wind power, however successfully it increases its share of electricity production. Some believe that wind will never produce enough power to be taken seriously. Others believe that all renewable energy sources must be explored and invested in to combat global warming. People are divided on the environmental effects of wind turbines, and in open landscapes. Many believe that wind farms are essential and should be accommodated in the best way possible; others disagree. The arguments for both sides given in this book will help you to make up your own mind.

Fluttering power

Closer to the ground, American inventors are working on using the 'aeroelastic flutter' or vibration caused by moving air to power micro-wind devices. They work by allowing a vibrating membrane to drive a mini-generator.

Glossary

anemometer   A device that measures wind speed.

carbon dioxide (CO_2)   A greenhouse gas given off when fossil fuels are burned.

carbon fibre   A strong, light synthetic material.

circulation   Free movement in a circular direction.

circumference   The distance around the boundary of a circle or sphere.

climate change   A change in general weather conditions over a long period of time, including higher temperatures, more or less rain, droughts, etc.

clipper   A fast sailing ship with tall masts and many sails.

cogwheel   A toothed wheel that fits together with another wheel to turn it.

continental shelf   The sloping underwater area near land at the edge of a continent.

deflect   To change the course of something.

drag   Resistance when moving through air.

dyke   An embankment built to hold back water and stop flooding.

dynamo   A machine that turns mechanical energy into electrical energy.

electricity grid   A large network of cables for transmitting electrical power.

electromagnetic radiation   The range of electrical and magnetic radiation given off by the Sun, which includes radio waves and visible light.

generator   A machine that turns mechanical energy into electrical energy.

glass fibre   Strong thread made by pulling molten glass through a narrow opening.

global warming   Heating up of the Earth's surface, especially caused by pollution from burning fossil fuels.

greenhouse effect   Warming of the Earth's surface especially caused by pollution from burning fossil fuels.

housing   A covering that protects machine parts.

hub   The central part of a rotor.

incandescent   Producing light from great heat.

knot   A unit for measuring speed (1 knot = 1.85 km/h).

meteorologist   A scientist who studies the weather.

nitrogen oxide   A colourless, poisonous gas.

non-renewable energy   Energy that is used up and cannot be replaced (from sources such as coal, gas, oil or uranium).

patent   A document giving an inventor the exclusive right to sell something.

polder   An area of land drained and reclaimed from the sea.

prefabricate   To make something in sections in a factory, ready to be assembled somewhere else.

prevailing wind   The most common wind direction in a particular place.

renewable energy or resources   Sources of energy that do not run out such as biomass, geothermal, solar, water and wind power.

rotation   Turning motion; spinning.

rotor   The spinning assembly and blades of a turbine.

sulphur dioxide (SO$_2$)   A poisonous gas given off by burning coal.

tariff   A fee; price charged.

trade wind   A tropical wind blowing towards the equator from the east.

turbine   A machine with rotating blades that turn a shaft.

turbulence   Gusty movements of air.

wind farm or park   A large number of wind turbines in one area.

windshaft   The shaft or pole to which the sails of a windmill are attached.

Websites

The World Wind Energy Association explains the history and technology of turbines
www.world-wind-energy.info

Statistics, plans and reports from the Global Wind Energy Council
www.gwec.net

The Danish Wind Industry Association on wind power, including a guided tour
www.windpower.org/en/tour.htm

Information on small wind turbines from the American Wind Energy Association
www.awea.org/smallwind

A tour of wind farms around the world
www.ilr.tu-berlin.de/WKA/windfarm.html

Information from the UK Sustainable Development Commission
www.sd-commission.org.uk/pages/wind.html

Index